★ ★ ★

John Adams

John Adams

Barbara Silberdick Feinberg

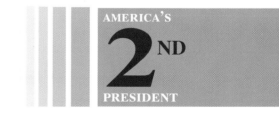

AMERICA'S

2ND

PRESIDENT

Children's Press®
A Division of Scholastic Inc.
New York / Toronto / London / Auckland / Sydney
Mexico City / New Delhi / Hong Kong
Danbury, Connecticut

Library of Congress Cataloging-in-Publication Data

Feinberg, Barbara.
    John Adams / by Barbara Silberdick Feinberg.
        p. cm. – (Encyclopedia of presidents)
    Summary: Details the coming of age, diplomatic and presidential career,
private life, and legacy of America's second president.
Includes bibliographical references and index.
    ISBN 0-516-22680-0
    1. Adams, John, 1735-1826—Juvenile literature. 2. Presidents—United
States—Biography—Juvenile literature. [1. Adams, John, 1735–1826.
2. Presidents.] I. Title. II. Series.
E322 .F54 2003
973.4'4'092—dc21   2002005895

CHILDREN'S PRESS and associated logos are trademarks and or registered
trademarks of Scholastic Library Publishing. SCHOLASTIC and associated
logos are trademarks and or registered trademarks of Scholastic Inc.
1 2 3 4 5 6 7 8 9 10 R 12 11 10 09 08 07 06 05 04 03

Contents

Chapter 1

Early Years

John Adams was born on October 30, 1735, to Deacon John Adams and Susanna Boylston Adams. Deacon John was a respected man in the town of Braintree, Massachusetts, 12 miles (19 kilometers) from Boston. Not only did he serve as a deacon (official) of his church, he was a member of the town council and a militiaman, who earned his living as a farmer and shoemaker. Susanna Boylston Adams came from a prominent family in Brookline. After young John's birth they had two more sons: Peter Boylston Adams, born in 1738, and Elihu Adams, born in 1741.

The Adams family could not dream that their son would grow up to be president of the United States. In 1735, there was no United States, and Massachusetts was still a British colony governed by a parliament and a king (George II) in faraway Great Britain. The

John Adams was born in this house on October 30, 1735. It has been preserved as part of the Adams National Historical Site in Quincy, Massachusetts.

Adamses wanted their eldest son to become a minister and thought their younger sons would become farmers.

John learned his ABCs at home in a six-room, two-story clapboard house. When he was about six years old, he went to a dame school, where classes were held in the teacher's home. The children learned reading and writing, beginning with simple books such as the *New England Primer*, which taught religious and moral values as well as reading.

When John was ten, he and the other children of Braintree watched the nearby shoreline, waiting fearfully for the French fleet to attack. Their fathers held military exercises on the town common, preparing to defend their homes. New England colonists and the British navy had captured the French fort at Louisbourg, Nova Scotia. The French navy threatened attacks along the New England coast. When news arrived that a storm at sea and widespread disease had scattered the French fleet, John and his neighbors gave thanks to God that the attack never came.

By this time, John was attending Braintree's Latin School, which was run by Joseph Cleverly. Students went to the Latin School for six to eight years, until they were ready for college. They studied Latin and Greek; rules of grammar; rhetoric, the study of eloquent speaking and writing; logic, or reasoning clearly; and arithmetic. John thought Mr. Cleverly was a boring teacher. He sometimes

A popular game during John Adams's boyhood was *quoits*. Players toss rings, trying to land them on a post.

sneaked away from school to hunt, fish, and hike, popular pastimes for New England children. He also played marbles and quoits (a ring-toss game), flew kites, wrestled, and skated on frozen ponds in the wintertime.

One day, John told his father that he wanted to quit school and learn to farm. His angry father replied, "Well, I will show you what it is to be a farmer." Early the next morning, they trudged through wet and muddy marshes to spend the day harvesting and bundling thatching (reeds used as roofing). At the end of the day, John was exhausted, but he claimed that he still liked being a farmer. His father insisted that he return to school. John admitted that it was the teacher, not the school that he disliked.

Soon John was studying with a tutor (a private teacher) named Joseph Marsh. Within a year and a half, the fifteen-year-old was ready to take the Harvard College admission exam. Marsh planned to travel with him to the college at Cambridge, but he got sick at the last minute. John had to travel to Cambridge by himself. Frightened and reluctant, he almost turned around and went home, but he did not want to disappoint his father. He passed the test and was granted a partial scholarship. "I was as light when I came home, as I had been heavy when I went," he wrote.

John Adams thrived at Harvard. After discovering the college library, he developed a lifelong passion for reading and collecting books. Adams admired Professor John Winthrop, who taught astronomy, and never forgot the thrill of looking through a telescope at the moons of Jupiter. At the end of his studies, in 1755, John graduated among the top three students in his class. He and his

This drawing of Harvard College from the early 1700s shows what it must have looked like when John Adams was a student there in the 1750s.

Harvard, founded in 1636, was the first college established in North America. In the 1750s, it occupied only four buildings and a chapel. Seven faculty members instructed about a hundred students in Latin, Greek, philosophy, mathematics, and science. Most students were training to be ministers in New England churches. John Adams's entering class contained twenty-seven young men, ranging from thirteen to twenty-two years old. No women were admitted. Harvard students came mostly from old New England families and were ranked according to their family's importance. Adams ranked fourteenth.

The daily routine was difficult. Students attended morning prayers at six o'clock. They went to classes and studied from eight until five, with a break for lunch. In the late afternoon, they went to chapel again. After a light supper at seven, they continued to study. To relieve the pressure of study, students played pranks on one another and on the faculty. Sometimes, they defied the college's rules. If they were caught, they could be fined, whipped, or expelled from the college.

☆ ★ ☆

teachers agreed that he was not cut out to be a minister. He decided, with his family's approval, to study to be a lawyer instead.

Legal Training

John's father had sold 10 acres (4 hectares) of land to help pay for his son's college education. Now, however, John had to earn money on his own to study law. He went to Worcester, Massachusetts, 60 miles (100 kilometers) from Braintree, to teach twelve boys and girls in a one-room schoolhouse. He did not enjoy his new job. In a letter to a friend, he complained, "I am certain that keeping this school any length of time, would make a base weed and ignoble shrub of me."

During his stay in Worcester, the French and Indian War, another conflict between Britain and France, was threatening the colonies. Many young men were enlisting to fight. Adams accepted an assignment to carry a military dispatch from Worcester to Newport, Rhode Island—a long but not particularly dangerous trip—but he did not participate in the fighting. He sometimes worried that he was a coward.

Law students in the American colonies learned by working for and studying with experienced lawyers. There were no law schools. In 1756, Adams arranged to study law at night with lawyer James Putnam while teaching children during the daytime. He paid Putnam a fee of $100 to read British law books and discuss them with him. The huge collections of laws and commentaries were dull stuff. "Can you imagine any drier reading?" he asked years later. He completed his studies in two years and moved back to Braintree to live with his family and practice law.

Adams was embarrassed to lose his first legal case because of his own carelessness. He confided to his diary, "Let me never undertake to draw a writt [*sic*] without sufficient time to examine and digest in my mind all the doubts, queries, objections that may arise." He did routine legal work for clients in small Massachusetts towns and observed successful attorneys to learn their courtroom techniques. Yet he was dissatisfied. He was eager to try cases in Boston, where he could make a name for himself.

Adams particularly admired James Otis. In 1761, Otis defended Boston merchants who smuggled foreign goods into the

Fast Facts

THE FRENCH AND INDIAN WAR

What: The North American part of the conflict known in Europe as the Seven Years' War

When: 1754–1763

Who: France and its American Indian allies versus Great Britain (in Europe, France was allied with Spain and Austria and Britain was allied with Prussia)

Where: British troops and colonial Virginians fought French forces for control of the Ohio Valley. British and New England colonists attacked French Canada.

Why: France and Great Britain were rivals for control of Europe and of colonies in Asia and North America.

Outcome: With the fall of Montreal in 1760, Great Britain defeated France in North America. In the Treaty of Paris (1763), France gave up claims to Canada and lands east of the Mississippi River. (The French had given New Orleans and their claims west of the Mississippi to Spain in 1762.)

How We Know What Adams Thought

We know more about what John Adams thought and felt than we know about many other important people of his time. While he was a student at Harvard, he started keeping a diary. In it, he described his feelings and frequently took stock of his character. He had trouble controlling his temper and felt that his biggest weakness was believing that he was always right.

Quincy July 7th 1812.

Dear Sir

If I were as rich as Mr Stephen Gerard or Mr William Grey, I would publish and proclaim offices and promises of Rewards in Gold and Silver, in Money and in Medals, for the best Essays on Several Subjects, Some of which I will now hint, without any regard to arrangement

1 100 Dollars or Eagles if I could afford them, and a gold Medal for the best History of our American Navy and its Exploits as well as of its rise and progress in 1775. 6. 7. 8. 9. 1780. 1. 2 and three.

2 Ditto for the best History of the American Navy in 1797. 8. 9. 1800. 1801. 1802

3. For the most compleat History of Gallatins Insurrection its rise progress, decline and Suppression.

4. Ditto for the best Relation in detail of the Motives causes views designs and

Later, Adams wrote thousands of letters to his wife and friends. The letters describe the events of his day as well as his personal thoughts and feelings. In retirement, he started composing an autobiography but never finished it. His family kept all of his papers and later published the diaries and letters, giving historians and biographers a detailed picture of his life and thoughts over more than fifty years.

☆ ★ ☆

country to avoid Britain's unfair trade restrictions and taxes. British customs officials enforced the laws using writs of assistance (general search warrants) to ransack people's homes and businesses, looking for evidence of smuggling. The merchants hired Otis to challenge the writs. He lost the case, but colonists began to repeat his arguments that Britain was violating their rights as British citizens.

In May 1761, John's father died during an influenza epidemic. He left John a house on the family property and about 40 acres (18 hectares) of farmland and orchard. John's brother Peter inherited the family home and most of the land. John wrote that his father was "the honestest [*sic*] man I ever knew." The desire to please his father was a source of John's ambition to make a name for himself.

Marriage of Hearts and Minds

In 1759, when he was twenty-three, John met fourteen-year-old Abigail Smith and her sisters, the daughters of Reverend William Smith and Elizabeth Quincy Smith of Weymouth. Abigail was a fragile child who received her education at home. She had many spare hours to read books in her father's library. Yet she also must have been spirited. John was not very impressed with the Smith sisters, writing that they were "Not fond, not frank, not candid." Two years later, John and Abigail met again. Adams, now a talkative young lawyer, was attracted to Abigail, who had become a charming and witty young woman.

At first, Abigail's parents were not happy about John and Abigail courting. Abigail was still only sixteen, and they may have thought she could find a man more important or richer than John Adams. However, they consented to the courtship. John and Abigail exchanged love letters, signing them with the classical names Lysander and Diana, a custom of the times. One of Abigail's letters

Vaccinations Against Smallpox

John postponed his wedding date with Abigail for several weeks so that he could be inoculated against smallpox. His legal work often took him to Boston, where there were frequent outbreaks of this very contagious disease. It spread from person to person and from contaminated clothes and bedding. Victims developed high fevers and a rash, or pox, on the skin, and at least 30 percent of them died.

In the 1760s, inoculation was done by deliberately infecting people with a weak strain of the variola virus that caused smallpox. They usually came down with a mild case of the disease, but gained lifelong immunity. Patients were quarantined, or kept away from others to avoid spreading the disease, for six weeks. They ate a diet of bland foods such as pudding, rice, bread, and milk. Many were left with smallpox scars on their faces. One out of every one hundred people vaccinated in this way died of the disease.

In 1796, British physician Edward Jenner discovered that inoculating people with cowpox, a much milder disease, also gave immunity to smallpox. Patients did not have to be quarantined and did not become ill. These improved smallpox vaccinations were routinely given to small children for more than 150 years.

☆ ★ ☆

A portrait of Abigail Adams as a young woman.

opened with the salutation "Dearest Friend," a greeting she would use for the rest of their lives. John wrote that she "always softened and warmed my heart."

On October 25, 1764, Reverend Smith, Abigail's father, united John and Abigail at the Weymouth meetinghouse before many friends and relatives. John was almost 29 years old and Abigail was about to turn 19. The couple moved to the house John inherited, a small gray clapboard cottage next to the house where John was born. Abigail settled in easily. John was frequently away pleading cases in distant courts or meeting with lawyers in Boston. She was not lonely because John's brother Peter and his family lived next door together with John and Peter's mother. Soon Abigail had a baby to care for. On July 14, 1765, she gave birth to the Adams's first child, a girl named Abigail whom they nicknamed Nabby.

John began to take up responsibilities in local government. In 1765, he was a surveyor of highways. During that year, the Stamp Act, a new tax imposed by Great Britain, created an outcry in the colonies. John got involved in heated discussions about it. His career would soon be moving to a larger stage.

Chapter 2

Rebellion in Massachusetts

In 1765, the British passed the Stamp Act, which required that all printed materials—legal documents, newspapers, and even playing cards—carry a stamp bought from the British government. The colonists were outraged at this new form of taxation, and they refused to buy the stamps. John Adams was personally affected. Courts could not conduct business without stamps on legal documents, so they closed.

Unable to work, Adams spent time writing a *Dissertation on the Canon and Feudal Law*. This historical work argued that citizens have natural (basic) rights that no church or state can take away. Readers recognized that Adams's arguments encouraged the colonists to defend their rights by challenging the British government. About the same time, the town of Braintree asked him to prepare a series of

instructions for their representative to the colonial legislature. Adams's instructions, which were reprinted in the *Boston Gazette,* demanded that the government recognize the colonists' rights as British citizens.

The people of Boston, impressed by Adams's arguments, asked him to help convince the governor and his council to reopen the courts without a stamp on legal documents. The governor referred the issue to the colony's judges. In January 1766, they agreed to reopen the courts. Meanwhile, news of the colonists' resistance to the Stamp Act had reached Britain. The British government chose to repeal the Stamp Act. News of this decision arrived in May. Adams summed it up this way:

> The year 1765 has been the most remarkable year of my life. That
>
> enormous engine, fabricated by the British Parliament for battening
>
> down all the rights and liberties of America, I mean the Stamp Act,
>
> has raised and spread through the whole continent a spirit that will
>
> be recorded to our honor with all future generations.

Colonists refused to buy the stamps. They organized demonstrations against the Stamp Act and attacked government workers who sold the stamps.

The title for a price list of British stamps to be placed on all parchment, writing paper, and printing paper.

STAMP-OFFICE,
Lincoln's-Inn, 1765.

A
TABLE

Of the Prices of Parchment and Paper for the Service of America.

Adams returned to his expanding law practice. In 1767, John and Abigail celebrated the arrival of their second child, a son whom they named John Quincy Adams. Adams moved his growing family to Boston to be nearer to the courts. A daughter, Susanna, was born in 1768.

The birthplace of John and Abigail's son John Quincy Adams, who became the sixth president. It stands near John Adams's birthplace (see page 8).

That year, Adams faced a difficult decision. The governor asked him to serve as advocate general in the Court of Admiralty, which heard cases concerning the law of the seas. It was an important position, but the advocate general was responsible for prosecuting Massachusetts citizens who defied Britain's taxes and shipping restrictions. The British Parliament had enacted the Townshend Acts, putting high taxes on tea, paint, lead, and glass. Adams decided to refuse the governor's appointment. He knew that many citizens would find ways to avoid the new taxes, and he did not want to be the person to prosecute them.

The campaign against the Townshend Acts was led by another Adams. Samuel Adams, John's cousin, wrote letters and pamphlets urging the people of Massachusetts to boycott (refuse to buy) taxed British goods. Citizens of Boston either went without tea and other taxed items or bought untaxed goods that were smuggled into the city. The British responded by sending troops into the city in a show of force. Bostonians asked John Adams to draft instructions for their legislators to protest the presence of these troops.

On March 5, 1770, alarm bells rang and news spread that British soldiers had fired on some Bostonians. A crowd in the city had threatened and jeered at a small group of soldiers and pelted them with snowballs. The troops fired on the crowd, and five people were killed. Captain Thomas Preston and eight of his men were arrested. The incident came to be known as the Boston Massacre.

The BLOODY MASSACRE perpetrated in King—Street BOSTON on March 5th 1770. by a party of the 29th REGT.

BUTCHERS HALL

Engrav'd Printed & Sold by PAUL REVERE BOSTON

British troops at right fire on Boston citizens at left. The illustration was engraved soon after the event by Paul Revere.

Together with two other Boston lawyers, John Adams volunteered to defend the soldiers. It was an unpopular cause, but Adams believed that every British citizen was entitled to a fair trial, even British soldiers. In court, he argued that they had acted in self-defense. He said, "Facts are stubborn things, and whatever may be our wishes, our inclinations, or the dictums of our passions, they cannot alter the state of facts and evidence." The jury acquitted Preston and six of his men. The other two were found guilty of manslaughter. They were branded on the thumbs as punishment. Adams's defense of the British soldiers seemed not to reduce his popularity. Later that year, he was elected as Boston's representative to the Massachusetts legislature.

Meanwhile, John and Abigail struggled to support and care for their family. In February 1770, the Adams's fourteen-month-old daughter Susanna died. Adams's grief was so great that for years, he refused to speak of her death. Later that year, Abigail gave birth to Charles Adams, and in September 1772, a third son, Thomas Boylston Adams, was born. Their family was complete.

In December 1773, a group of Bostonians, disguised as Indians, boarded British ships in the Boston Harbor and threw chests of taxed tea into the water. Known as the Boston Tea Party, the nighttime raid infuriated the British. Adams usually deplored mob action, but even he seemed to approve of this

Boston patriots returning from British merchant ships in the harbor after their "tea party" in 1773 — they dumped chests of heavily taxed British tea into the water.

Sam Adams: Rebel

Samuel Adams (1722–1803), John Adams's cousin, grew up in Boston. After graduating from Harvard College in 1740, Sam failed as a brewer, a newspaper publisher, and a tax collector. By the 1760s, he was deeply in debt and had trouble supporting his growing family. Yet Sam was a political activist who had an instinctive under-

Samuel Adams, a leader of the patriots in Boston and organizer of the Boston Tea Party. He was a cousin of John Adams.

standing of people and politics.

During the Stamp Act crisis of 1765, he organized Bostonians and small-town farmers to protest the new tax on printed materials. Later, he organized the Sons of Liberty, a group of daring men willing to demonstrate against the British. He also set up committees of correspondence which kept in touch with activists in other American colonies. In 1773, he coordinated the Boston Tea Party. From 1774 to 1781, he served on many committees of the Continental Congress. He signed the Declaration of Independence and later helped rally support for the Constitution. He served as governor of Massachusetts from 1794 to 1797.

☆★☆

demonstration. He wrote, "This destruction of the tea is so bold, so daring, so firm, intrepid, and inflexible, and it must have so important consequences . . ." Britain retaliated by passing the Coercive Acts, which closed the port of Boston. The people of Boston closed the courts in response. As a result, Adams had little legal work to do.

The Continental Congresses

In 1774, the governments of the North American colonies agreed to meet in Philadelphia, the leading colonial city, to discuss the crisis with Great Britain. They called the gathering the Continental Congress. The Massachusetts legislature sent John and Samuel Adams and other delegates to the meeting. John Adams wrote in his diary, "I feel myself unequal to this business. A more extensive knowledge of the realm, the colonies, and of commerce as well as of law and policy, is necessary than I am the master of." He had never before been outside New England. He wrote to his wife, "There is in Congress a collection of the greatest men upon this continent in point of abilities, virtues, and fortunes."

Massachusetts had suffered most from harsh British treatment, and its delegates were in favor of taking strong measures. The other delegates were sympathetic to Massachusetts, but they were not ready to declare their independence from Britain. They wanted to negotiate with Britain. The meetings dragged on for days. Adams complained, "In Congress, nibbling and quibbling as usual. There is no greater mortification [disgrace] than to sit with half a dozen witts [*sic*], deliberating upon a petition, address, or memorial."

Adams and the Massachusetts delegation did get some help from the Continental Congress. It agreed to support Massachusetts's resistance to the Coercive Acts and to not import, export, or buy British goods after September 1775. The delegates left for home at the end of October. That winter, Adams wrote the *Novanglus* (New Englander) articles. In them, he argued that the colonies were self-governing states within the British Empire. Because the colonies were not represented in Parliament, that legislature could only regulate the colonies' overseas trading if the colonies consented.

In April 1775, British troops marched from Boston to the villages of Concord and Lexington to seize arms and ammunition from the colonists. Local militias, called Minutemen because they pledged to be ready to fight at a minute's notice, defended themselves by firing on the British. These skirmishes are often considered the first battles of the Revolutionary War.

Only a month later, John Adams and his fellow delegates were in Philadelphia again to attend the Second Continental Congress. Adams knew that Massachusetts could not go to war by itself, and other colonies seemed reluctant to fight. To encourage the delegates to work together, he suggested that a single

An artist's conception of the battle at Concord, Massachusetts, in April 1775, the first major battle of the Revolutionary War.

Continental Army be organized and that George Washington, a Virginian, be named commander in chief. Washington was an imposing figure who had fought bravely with the British against the French in the French and Indian War. Congress agreed.

Some delegates, led by John Dickinson of Pennsylvania, still hoped for reconciliation with Britain. They wrote the "Olive Branch Petition," asking the king to cancel the Coercive Acts. Adams signed the petition, but in private letters to his wife and a friend, he criticized Dickinson and the others. British troops

Staying in Touch

In John Adams's lifetime, mail delivery was slow and uncertain. Letters traveled by sea in sailing ships through unpredictable winds and weather or were carried by horseback over poorly built roads. It took six to nine days for a letter sent from Boston to arrive in New York City and at least a month to travel from Massachusetts to Georgia. Mail to and from Europe was even slower. Ships sailing from Great Britain to the colonies took four to six weeks to make the journey, and there was always the danger of a shipwreck or damage from leaking water.

During the Revolutionary War, there was another danger—the enemy could intercept and read mail. Adams was only embarrassed when his private letters were published, but he knew that a letter might reveal military or political secrets as well. In February 1779, when traveling to Europe, he wrote to Abigail, "So many vessels [*sic*] are taken, and there are so many Persons indiscreet, and so many others inquisitive, that I may not write."

☆★☆

seized these letters and published them. Adams was embarrassed, and for a long time Dickinson would not speak to him.

During the Congress, Adams attended meetings from seven in the morning to ten at night and chaired twenty-five committees while serving on many others. Military affairs were his main interest. As a chairman of the Board of War, he found ways to supply the Continental Army with food and munitions. He also pressed Congress to create a navy. By the end of the year, the colonies had seven ships and thirteen more in the planning stages. The delegates also adopted rules Adams drafted to govern the new fleet.

Fortunately, Congress adjourned from time to time, so Adams could return to Braintree to see his family. During his absences, Abigail ran the farm, cared for the children's health and education, and coped with many crises, including the death of her mother. She still found time to write to her husband and tell him about Massachusetts politics as well as family matters.

Independence

In June 1776, Congress appointed Adams to a committee on independence, which was to draft a declaration for its approval. He encouraged Thomas Jefferson, a committee member from Virginia, to write the document. In his *Autobiography*, Adams explained that "I had a great opinion of the Elegance of his pen, and none

A draft copy of the Declaration of Independence written by Thomas Jefferson with revisions made by John Adams and Benjamin Franklin.

The committee that prepared the Declaration presents it to the Continental Congress. John Adams is at the left, and Jefferson is fourth from the left.

at all of my own." When Adams led the final debate on independence, Jefferson remarked, "John Adams was our Colossus on the floor. He was not graceful nor elegant, nor remarkably fluent but he came out occasionally with a power of thought and expression that moved us from our seats." Adams could be blunt and outspoken, but no one doubted his patriotism or his honesty.

After Congress voted for independence on July 2, Adams wrote jubilantly to Abigail:

> The Second Day of July will be the most memorable epocha,[sic] in the History of America. —I am apt to believe that it will be celebrated, by succeeding Generations, as the great anniversary festival . . . It ought to be solemnized with pomp and parade, with shews [shows], games, sports, guns, bells, bonfires, and illuminations from one end of this continent to the other from this time forward forever more.

Adams was off by two days. The Declaration was not formally adopted until July 4, the date we now celebrate as Independence Day. An official copy was not ready for the delegates' signatures until August.

Even as the Congress was busy conducting the war against British troops, it began drafting a document describing how the colonies would work together in the future. Adams took part in some of the debates over these Articles of Confederation. They were finally ratified (approved) and went into effect in 1781.

During 1776 and 1777, Adams concentrated on the way the new union of colonies would deal with other nations. As a member of the committee on treaties, he studied English treaties and trade agreements and drafted a sample commercial treaty with France. This interest in foreign affairs soon led to a new and exciting chapter in his life.

Chapter 3

Commissioner to France ────────────

The war went badly for the colonies in 1776 and 1777. British troops withdrew from Boston, but soon afterward they occupied New York and drove George Washington's army out of New Jersey. In September 1777, they occupied Philadelphia.

That same month, there came a ray of hope. In a series of major battles, American colonists defeated a British army in the Hudson Valley, forcing its surrender at Saratoga, New York. Hope increased that other European nations would recognize the country and provide support against the British.

On November 28, Congress appointed Adams as a commissioner to France to represent the United States. Abigail longed to join her husband, but the trip across the Atlantic was dangerous, especially in the winter and in wartime. They decided that only John and ten-year-old John Quincy would risk the voyage. On February 13, 1778, father and son left on the frigate *Boston*. They were pursued by British warships, came under fire, and survived a violent storm that split the main mast, but they landed safely in Bordeaux, France, on April 1.

Adams was amazed by how luxuriously the French ruling classes lived. Although he had traveled to Boston, New York, and Philadelphia, he described himself as "a poor man almost without a name, unknown in the European world, born and educated in the American wilderness, out of which he had never set foot until 1778."

Arriving in Paris, he was disgusted to see the other American commissioners living like wealthy Frenchmen. He stayed at first with Commissioner Benjamin Franklin, but he disapproved of Franklin, who spent many afternoons and evenings at parties entertaining the ladies. Franklin was widely admired by the French for his scientific experiments and his writings, and Adams may have been jealous of the older man's fame. Adams helped by putting all the commissioners' accounts in order and paying overdue bills. He also handled correspondence with Congress and studied the French language. After less than a year, Adams learned that Franklin had been named minister to France, so he decided to return home. He had learned much about European ways, but felt that he had not accomplished very much.

Benjamin Franklin (standing) enjoyed the glittering social life of Paris. John Adams found such social gatherings a waste of time and money.

A Constitution for Massachusetts ───────

Adams had hardly gotten settled at home when Massachusetts called a convention to write a new state constitution. The Braintree town meeting asked him to represent them at the convention. He wrote the main draft of the document, and it was adopted with only a few changes. He provided for a two-house legislature elected by property owners and for a strong governor assisted by a council. The constitution also had a bill of rights—a list of rights belonging to the people—which, unlike most of the other state charters, included freedom of assembly.

Diplomatic Missions in Europe ───────

Adams spent only 104 days in Massachusetts. Congress had asked him to return to Paris to help prepare for a peace conference with Britain to end the war in North America. This time, he sailed for Europe with John Quincy, now twelve years old, and Charles, almost ten. He enrolled his sons in school in Paris and began to discuss peace terms with the French foreign minister Vergennes. Adams learned that the French wanted to control the negotiations with Britain, and he believed this was unacceptable. Besides, the British were not yet ready to hold the talks. Adams had almost nothing to do, and he became irritable.

Finally, he took his sons out of school and traveled with them to the Netherlands. There he got to know leaders in the Dutch government. With the approval of Congress, he became the spokesman for United States in the Netherlands. Over the next two years, the Dutch agreed to recognize the United States as an independent country and to give the new nation a loan. Adams also shopped for small luxury items that were difficult to find in North America. He sent them to Abigail, who sold them at a profit to help support the family. At first, John Quincy and Charles became students at the famous University of Leyden. Then John Quincy was offered a chance to travel to Russia as the secretary to the American minister. Charles, who missed Massachusetts, returned to Braintree.

Fast Facts

AMERICAN REVOLUTION

What: Also known as the War of Independence

When: 1776–1783

Who: Great Britain against the thirteen North American colonies, which were aided by France, the Netherlands, and Spain

Where: In the thirteen North American colonies and in the Atlantic Ocean

Why: British internal taxes and trade policies violated colonists' rights, so the colonists asserted their independence. The British found this unacceptable.

Outcome: Treaty of Paris (1783) in which Britain recognized the independence of the American states, confirmed American fishing rights off Newfoundland, and ceded territory between the Appalachian Mountains and the Mississippi River. The United States agreed to try to end ill treatment of colonists who remained loyal to Britain by state and local governments and to restore property that had been taken from the loyalists during the war.

While Adams was in the Netherlands, the Revolutionary War came to a close with the surrender of British general Charles Cornwallis in October 1781. His defeat ended British hopes for ruling the American colonies. At long last, the British were ready to negotiate a peace treaty.

In late 1782, Adams returned to Paris, joining Franklin and John Jay to discuss peace terms with the British. Adams spoke on behalf of New England's fishing fleets, and Britain agreed to protect the right of the fleets to fish off Canadian shores. He also supported the rights of American and British businessmen to collect debts that had been left unpaid during the war. Adams also insisted that the British make large concessions of land in the West. The final treaty conceded all land east of the Mississippi River to the United States, giving the country room to grow. The Treaty of Paris was signed in September 1783. While waiting for Congress to ratify the treaty, John and John Quincy toured Britain, and John had his portrait painted in London.

The signature page of the Treaty of Paris, which ended the Revolutionary War. It has the red wax seals and signatures of American negotiators John Adams, Benjamin Franklin, and John Jay.

Article 10.

The solemn Ratifications of the present Treaty expedited in good and due Form shall be exchanged between the contracting Parties in the Space of six Months or sooner, if possible, to be computed from the Day of the Signature of the Present Treaty In Witness whereof We the undersigned their Ministers Plenipotentiary have in their Name and in Virtue of our full Powers, signed with our Hands the present Definitive Treaty, and caused the Seals of our Arms to be affixed thereto.

Done at Paris, this third Day of September In the Year of our Lord, one thousand, seven hundred and Eighty three.

D Hartley

John Adams.

B Franklin

John Jay

Painter John Singleton Copley

The portrait of John Adams painted by American John Singleton Copley in London.

John Singleton Copley (1738–1815), raised in Boston, was America's first great portrait artist. His stepfather, Peter Pelham, taught him to paint and engrave. Paul Revere, Samuel Adams, and John Hancock were among the men who posed for him. In 1766, Copley sent a painting to a British exhibition that won him an invitation to join the Royal Academy of Arts in Great Britain. In 1775, he settled in England, where he spent the rest of his life, painting mostly biblical and historical scenes.

In 1783, he painted John Adams's portrait. Copley showed him as a statesman, standing next to a globe and table of maps. Adams did not like the portrait because he thought he looked too arrogant and self-assured.

Ambassador

Adams remained in Europe, negotiating further treaties and loan agreements with the Netherlands and France. In 1784, he learned that he would be appointed the first United States minister to Great Britain. He asked Abigail and eighteen-year-old Nabby to join him. While they waited for the official appointment, the family took a house in Auteuil, a suburb of Paris. John Quincy, recently returned from Russia, prepared himself to return to Massachusetts and attend Harvard. The family spent happy times with Thomas Jefferson, then the United States minister in France. The Adamses moved to Britain in 1785 when John's appointment was officially announced. In London, they continued their friendship with Jefferson by giving his daughter Polly (Mary) a place to stay when she first arrived from Virginia.

On June 1, 1785, Adams was formally presented to King George III. Soon after the occasion he wrote a letter to John Jay, secretary of foreign affairs for the Confederation, reporting on the ceremony. "The King listened to every word I said, with dignity but without apparent emotion," he noted. Then he described his private audience with the British monarch. He said that George III's speech was filled with so many hesitations that Adams could not be sure of his exact words. George III was known to stutter.

King George III of Great Britain was the monarch against whom the American colonies rebelled. John Adams, the first minister of the United States to Britain, was presented to the king in 1785.

The king said, "There is an opinion among some people that you are not the most attached of all your countrymen to the manners of France."

Adams replied, "I must avow to your Majesty, I have no attachment but to my own country."

"An honest man will never have any other," the king answered. He bowed indicating that their interview was over.

"I retreated, stepping backwards, as is the etiquette," Adams concluded, "and, making my last reverence [bow] at the door of the chamber, I went my way."

Within six months, however, Adams was disappointed once again. Even though the two countries had signed a peace treaty, neither side was willing to carry out all of its terms. Adams realized that "No step that I can take, no language I can hold, will do any good, or, indeed, much harm."

Outside his formal duties, Adams learned that the leading men of Britain had little interest in him or in the United States. He had time to time tour Britain and entertain American visitors. Nabby broke off an engagement to a young man in Massachusetts. Later, she fell in love with her father's secretary, Colonel William Stephens Smith. The young couple was married with the approval of John and Abigail.

In 1786, Adams began work on *A Defence of the Constitutions.* He studied the constitutions of modern Switzerland and the American states as well as those of ancient republics. As in his draft for the constitution of Massachusetts, he recommended a two-house legislature. This book and his other writings on government became his contribution to the preparation of the United States

The United States Constitution

The Constitutional Convention met in Philadelphia in 1787 to replace the Articles of Confederation with a plan that would create a stronger federal government. As Adams would have liked, the delegates created a legislature with two houses—the Senate and the House of Representatives. They also provided for independent national courts and an executive to carry out the work of governing. Each of these governmental branches had powers that were checked or balanced by other branches. The Constitution also made clear that laws passed by the new federal government would be superior to state laws and that they could be applied directly to the people. The national government would have power to raise its own funds and to enforce its laws.

When John Adams read about the new Constitution in London, he was surprised that it had no bill (or declaration) of rights, like those in the Massachusetts and Virginia constitutions. He wrote to Thomas Jefferson in France, "What think you of a Declaration of Rights? Should not such a thing have preceded the model?" Many others also wanted a bill of rights, and the framers agreed to add it after the Constitution was ratified by the states. The Bill of Rights was added to the Constitution in 1791 as the first ten amendments.

☆ ☆ ☆

Constitution. When the Constitutional Convention met in 1787, Adams was still in England, unable to participate in the deliberations. However, his ideas were familiar to many of the delegates there.

Triumphal Return

Disappointed with his mission to Britain, Adams and his family set sail for Boston in the spring of 1788. After ten years abroad, Adams looked ahead to a quieter role within his home state. He thought he might take up his long abandoned law practice and didn't expect to serve his nation again.

To his great surprise, the citizens of Boston arranged a gala welcome when he and Abigail arrived in port on June 17. Church bells pealed, and cannons boomed. After a reception, the Adamses were invited to stay in Governor John Hancock's mansion while renovations were completed on their new home, Peacefield. They had bought this 83-acre property before they left London. It was only a mile from their old home in Braintree. There, it seemed, they could settle down at last.

Chapter 4

The First Presidential Election ———

On June 21, 1788, only four days after John and Abigail Adams arrived back in Massachusetts, New Hampshire became the ninth state to ratify the new Constitution. This meant that the Constitution became effective, replacing the Articles of Confederation and setting in motion plans for the first presidential election. Unexpectedly, Adams found himself called to serve his nation once again.

Supporters of the new Constitution agreed that George Washington should be elected the nation's first president. Washington and his advisers agreed that the vice president should come from a northern state to encourage national unity. John Adams was the obvious choice. Adams agreed to be a candidate. In November, people in each state chose members of the electoral college (the group that actually voted for president). These electors assembled in early 1789 and cast their ballots for Washington and Adams to serve as the nation's first president and vice president.

Adams, short and stout and known for his intellectual arguments, provided quite a contrast to Washington, the tall, distinguished former general, who was already considered "The Father of His Country." Once they were elected, the two men and their wives moved to New York City, the temporary capital of the United States. Adams arrived before Washington and was sworn in by the president pro tempore of the Senate, the senator serving as temporary presiding officer.

Presidential Elections 1789–1793

Article II, Section One of the U.S. Constitution required electors in each state to choose the president and vice president. They each were to cast two ballots for president. One of the two votes had to be for a candidate living outside the elector's state. The candidate who won the most votes became president; the second-place finisher became vice president. Some of these provisions were changed later by a constitutional amendment.

In the election of 1788–89, there were 69 electors. George Washington received 69 votes and was elected president unanimously. The electors split their second votes among many candidates. John Adams received 34, far more than any of the others, so he was elected vice president. Four years later, in 1792–93, Washington was reelected with 133 electoral votes, and Adams continued as vice president with 77.

☆☆☆

George Washington is sworn in as first president in New York on April 30, 1789. Vice President Adams is at the right.

Life in New York was good to the Adamses. They rented an elegant mansion named Richmond Hill, near the Hudson River a mile or so north of the city. The new vice president enjoyed the recognition he received as a government dignitary. Also, John and Abigail were often invited to the Washingtons' social receptions. Best of all, the Adamses were able to visit frequently with Nabby and her children, who lived on Long Island.

In November 1790, federal government moved to Philadelphia, the new temporary capital of the United States. John and Abigail rented Bush Hill, a mansion outside the city, and their sons Thomas and Charles lived with them, while John Quincy remained in Boston where he was practicing law. Keeping up two households on John's $5,000 salary became too expensive, so Abigail began to spend more and more time at the family home in Quincy.

Adams soon learned that the vice president had few powers. If a president died, the vice president would become president. Otherwise, his only official duties were to preside over the Senate and cast the deciding vote in the event of a tie. In a letter to Abigail, Adams described the vice presidency as "the most insignificant office that ever the Invention of Man contrived or his Imagination conceived."

When he presided over the Senate, Adams's own behavior did not help his cause. In the beginning, he actively participated in the debates. During the first

A view of Philadelphia about the time the national government moved there from New York.

session, he irritated the senators by stating his own views about titles. He joined the debate on how people should address the president of the United States and proposed the greeting "Your Majesty." He felt such a formal title would bring dignity and respect to the new federal government in its dealings with the states and with older, more established nations. The senators found this too monarchical. They began to make fun of the vice president and privately called him "His Rotundity" and the "Duke of Braintree."

Finally, the Senate decided that the vice president should not be permitted to speak, ending his ability to contribute to the debates. He wrote disconsolately to Abigail, "It is sure a punishment to hear other men talk five hours every day and not be at liberty to talk at all myself as more than half I hear appears to me very young, inconsiderate, and inexperienced."

Adams could still cast a deciding ballot when a Senate vote ended in a tie. He broke more than thirty-one ties in his eight years as vice president. The most important of these confirmed President Washington's power to remove officials he appointed, thereby blocking attempts to weaken presidential power. Adams cast five of his tie-breaking votes in support of a crucial compromise between northern and southern states. Northerners wanted the federal government to pay the Revolutionary War debts of their state governments. Southern states wanted the permanent capital to be located in or near the South. New Yorker Alexander Hamilton and Virginian Thomas Jefferson arranged a compromise. If southerners would vote for the payment of war debts, northerners would agree to plan a new capital city on the border between northern and southern states. Maryland and Virginia agreed to contribute the land for a new District of Columbia. Many senators on both sides were against any compromise, so the vote on the proposal was tied. Adams cast the deciding vote in favor, and the proposal passed. Later, he would be the first president to serve in the new capital, originally named Federal City, but soon renamed Washington.

Vice President Adams did not advise President Washington and was not part of his Cabinet. Because the vice president's main responsibility was to preside over the Senate, Washington and Adams thought of the vice presidency as a part of the legislative branch. They did not want to violate separation of powers by having frequent consultations. At the time, the Senate met for only a few months each year, so Adams was left with little to do. In his second term, he often traveled back to Massachusetts when Congress was not meeting. On one important matter, Washington wrote, "Presuming that the Vice-President will have left the seat of the government for Boston, I have not requested his opinion to be taken."

The French Revolution

As a longtime diplomat, Adams took a keen interest in Europe. In 1789, only months after he became vice president, the people of France revolted against the French monarchy. Soon the Revolution became violent. Thousands (including the king and queen) were put to death, and normal government and business activities came to a standstill.

As he had done during the American Revolution, Adams wrote a historical essay, "Discourse on Davila." It was about earlier civil wars in France during the 1500s, but the argument seemed to be about current events. Adams favored "the monarchical principle" as a balance against the unpredictable forces of democracy. Adams's enemies accused him of wanting a king in the United States, but he was arguing that a strong executive—such as President Washington—was important in a republican government to preserve law and order.

In 1793, King Louis XVI of France receives a last blessing before revolutionary leaders cut off his head in the *guillotine* at the right.

In private, Thomas Jefferson wrote some very negative comments about Adams's essay, which were soon printed in public without his permission. Jefferson apologized to Adams, but Adams was badly hurt. Even though they were old friends, Adams and Jefferson had strong disagreements about political theory and practice. Jefferson warmly welcomed the French Revolution and its ideas of personal liberty and rule by the people. Adams was shocked by the revolution's bloody violence and the breakdown of law and order.

During Adams's second term as vice president, people with different views formed political parties. Many in the administration, led by Secretary of the Treasury Alexander Hamilton, came to be known as Federalists. They were friendly to Britain and believed the United States should remain neutral in the growing conflict between Britain and France. Like Adams, they favored a strong central government and wanted the United States to become a powerful commercial and manufacturing nation.

Those who opposed the Federalists came to be known as Democratic-Republicans. Secretary of State Thomas Jefferson was one of their leaders, and they were strong supporters of the French Revolution. They wanted to keep the United States a nation of independent farmers and to limit the role of the central government. Disagreements became so intense that both Hamilton and Jefferson resigned from President Washington's cabinet.

Alexander Hamilton, leader of the Federalists, became an adversary of John Adams and worked against his reelection in 1800.

President of the United States

In 1796, George Washington announced that he would not run for a third term as president. He was discouraged by the growing conflict between political parties. After many years of service, he wanted to retire to his home, Mount Vernon, on the Potomac River not far from the planned new capital.

Federalists assumed that John Adams would be the logical man to follow Washington in the presidency and nominated him for the post. In the popular election of 1796, the majority of voters supported the Federalists. However, not all Federalists supported Adams wholeheartedly. Party leader Alexander Hamilton preferred Adams's running mate, Thomas Pinckney, for president and suggested that some electors withhold their votes for Adams. Adams's supporters asked electors to vote for Adams but *not* for Pinckney.

When the electors met and their votes were tallied, the results were surprising. Adams won the presidency with 71 votes—nearly all Federalist electors cast one vote for him. Democratic-Republican leader Thomas Jefferson came in second with 68 votes! Federalist Pinckney came in third with only 59. So Adams began his presidency with Thomas Jefferson, the leader of the opposing party, as his vice president.

The States During the Presidency of John Adams

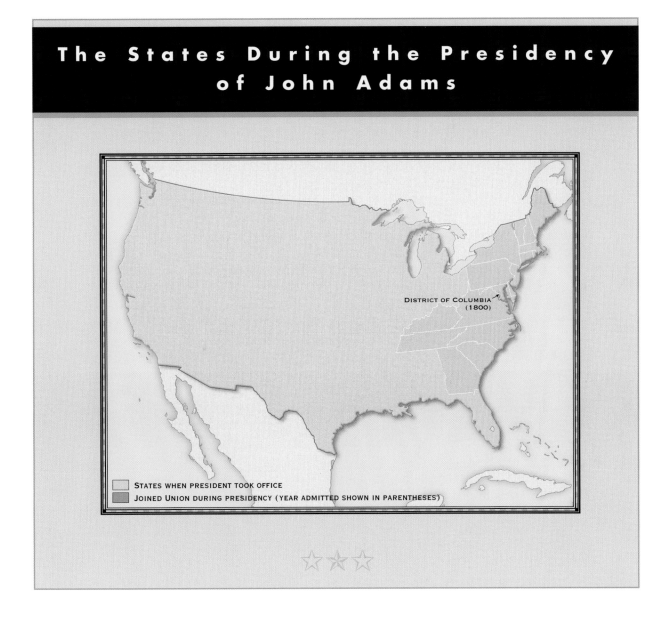

DISTRICT OF COLUMBIA
(1800)

STATES WHEN PRESIDENT TOOK OFFICE

JOINED UNION DURING PRESIDENCY (YEAR ADMITTED SHOWN IN PARENTHESES)

John Adams was the first vice president to be elected president of the United States. He was the only president to be sworn into office in Philadelphia (although Washington had begun his second term there). His inauguration on March 4, 1797, was the first of many peaceful transfers of power between U.S. presidents. This was an especially emotional occasion because George Washington, who had meant so much to the country, was retiring. Privately, Adams confessed that he was nervous about his new responsibilities.

Dressed in a new gray suit, with a sword strapped to his side and his hair powdered white, he gave his inaugural address, including these words: "If national pride is ever justifiable or excusable it is when it springs, not from power or riches, grandeur or glory, but from conviction of national innocence, information, and benevolence [kindness]." From Adams's personal point of view, duty had summoned him, and once more, he had answered. He would be receiving a yearly salary of $25,000, the largest sum he ever earned as a public servant.

One of his first acts in office was to meet with Thomas Jefferson. He suggested that they conduct the government in a nonpartisan fashion, giving up the intense party politics of the past few years. Jefferson discussed the suggestion with James Madison, another Democratic-Republican leader, and then (perhaps with some regret) refused Adams's offer.

Like Washington, Adams was a Federalist but as president, he too chose to rise above parties. Out of loyalty to President Washington, Adams kept on the members of his strongly Federalist cabinet. Adams learned too late that these heads of departments were more loyal to Federalist party leader Alexander Hamilton than they were to the president.

War with France?

Foreign relations dominated the Adams administration. Britain and France had gone to war in 1793. Many ordinary Americans sided with the French, who had declared a new republican government. However, merchants were being ruined because both British and French navies were capturing American ships on the high seas. Under President Washington, the Federalists pushed through the Jay Treaty with Britain, which reduced chances of war against Britain but deeply angered the French government and Democratic-Republicans at home.

Now the Federalists wanted Adams to go to war against France, and the Democratic-Republicans wanted him to side with France against the British. Adams chose instead to send three commissioners to France to find a diplomatic solution to the problems. The commissioners arrived in France in 1797 and were refused an audience with the foreign minister, Charles Talleyrand. As they waited, three shadowy agents approached the commissioners and offered to arrange a meeting with Talleyrand if the United States would first pay a bribe of $250,000 and then make a $12-million loan to France. The commissioners were outraged and refused.

Adams received the commissioners' report in early 1798. His first impulse was to ask Congress to declare war on France, and to prepare for war, he asked the legislature to pay to arm American ships. When Democratic-Republican members refused his request, he made the dispatches public, changing only the names of the French agents to X, Y, and Z. Congress was outraged by France's behavior. It quickly approved Adams's request for funds to arm ships.

As a result of the XYZ Affair, the returning commissioners were treated as heroes and toasted with the slogan "Millions for defense, but not one cent for tribute!" Adams enjoyed great, if temporary, popularity as the "Quasi-War" with France began. He proposed, and Congress agreed, to establish a Department of the Navy and the U.S. Marine Corps. He called George Washington back to duty as commander in chief of a new army. Washington requested that Adams name Alexander Hamilton as second in command, and Adams reluctantly agreed. As leader of the pro-British High Federalists, Hamilton was eager to go to war with France. He helped Adams push a bill through Congress to raise taxes to support the military.

A cartoon published in 1798 shows France, portrayed as a five-headed monster, demanding a bribe from the three American commissioners to France. They refuse to pay.

The Alien and Sedition Acts ───────────

As war with France seemed more likely, people became concerned about national security. In 1798, Congress passed a series of bills known as the Alien and Sedition Acts, and President Adams signed them into law. The Naturalization Act required aliens to live in the United States for fourteen years, not five, before applying for citizenship. The Alien Enemies Act allowed noncitizens to be deported if the United States was at war with their homeland and they were thought to endanger the security of the United States. Under the Alien Friends Act, noncitizens could be imprisoned or expelled from the country at any time by order of the president if he even *suspected* they might be wrongdoers. All these acts raised suspicion of Americans not born in the United States. Democratic-Republicans thought the acts were aimed at them, since some of their leading members were recent immigrants.

The Sedition Act made it a criminal offense for citizens to assemble to protest government policies. They could be fined $5,000 (a huge sum at that time) and sent to prison for five years. It became illegal for anyone to print, say, or publish any "false, scandalous, and malicious writing" against the government or the president. Those found guilty could be fined $2,000 and sentenced to two years in prison. Twenty-five men were charged under the sedition laws, and ten were convicted, most of them Democratic-Republican newspaper writers and editors.

Thus the nation's opposition party was temporarily silenced. Kentucky and Virginia passed resolutions declaring the sedition laws invalid because they denied freedoms guaranteed by the Bill of Rights. Fortunately, the Sedition Act was only temporary; it expired in 1800.

Adams knew that a war with France would be popular, and he knew that if he didn't take strong actions against France, the Federalist Party would suffer. Yet he did not want to go to war. Learning that French foreign minister Talleyrand was ready to negotiate, Adams appointed Democratic-Republican William Vans Murray as minister to France in 1799. Hamilton and the Federalists were furious that he did not send a Federalist. Secretary of State Timothy Pickering even defied Adams's requests to draft a treaty with France.

Then, on December 14, 1799, George Washington died. Freed from a sense of obligation to Washington, Adams removed Hamilton from command of the army, fired his Federalist cabinet, and sent William Vans Murray to France. Most moderate Federalists supported Adams. Murray and Talleyrand prepared a treaty, known as the Convention of 1800, ending the threat of war with France. It was ratified by the Senate. Adams considered the treaty one of the greatest accomplishments of his administration.

Time was running out on Adams's term. As the election of 1800 approached, the Federalist Party was split. Hamilton schemed to prevent Adams from being reelected and wrote a bitter pamphlet denouncing Adams's character. In his *Autobiography*, Adams later wrote, "Although I have long since forgiven this arch enemy, yet vice, folly, and villainy are not to be forgotten. . . ."

In November, Adams received disappointing news about the election. It appeared that the Democratic-Republicans had elected more members of the

The White House in 1800

When John and Abigail Adams moved into the Executive Mansion, only six of the thirty rooms could be used. The rest was still under construction. The Adamses lived among workmen who were building staircases and plastering walls. Water had to be hauled a mile from the nearest source. There was no indoor plumbing.

Abigail Adams wrote to Nabby, "The House is upon a grand and superb scale, requiring about thirty servants to attend and keep the apartments in proper order. . . . To assist us in this great castle, . . . bells are wholly wanting, not a single one being hung . . ." The Adamses had only four servants, and without bells, they had to shout when they wanted one of them to come.

"We have not the least fence, yard, or other conveniences without," Abigail complained to her sister, "and the great unfinished audience room [the East Room] I make a drying-room of, to hang clothes in." The Mansion was so damp that fires were lit in the fireplaces day and night (which is why Abigail could use a room to dry laundry).

☆ ★ ☆

electoral college than the Federalists. The outcome of the elections, however, would not be known for sure until the electors met and cast their votes in early 1801.

Just after the election, Adams moved to Washington, D.C., to spend the remaining months of his presidency in the new Executive Mansion (later known as the White House). On his first night in the house, he wrote a letter to Abigail

An early view of the Executive Mansion (later called the White House). When John and Abigail Adams moved in, the building was still unfinished.

that contained the following words: "I pray to heaven to bestow the best of blessings on this house and all that shall hereafter inhabit it. May none but honest and wise men ever rule under this roof." These words were later carved into a mantel in the State Dining Room and can be read there to this day.

Soon afterward, Abigail arrived.

Taking Leave

When the electoral college met, the Democratic-Republicans won the election. Two of their candidates, Thomas Jefferson and Aaron Burr, received 73 votes. Adams received only 65. Because Jefferson and Burr were tied, the election was thrown in to the House of Representatives. It eventually elected Jefferson as president and Burr as vice president.

President Adams made some appointments to the federal courts during the last months of his term. His political enemies called them "midnight judges," suggesting that it was unfair for a president to make long-term appointments when he knew he had been voted out of office. One of these judges had a lasting effect on the United States. He was John Marshall, then serving as secretary of state, whom Adams nominated to be chief justice of the Supreme Court. Marshall established the Court as a major force in the government of the United States and served until 1835.

On March 4, Adams left Washington at four o'clock in the morning on a coach to Massachusetts. Later that day, Thomas Jefferson was sworn in as the third president. Adams apparently saw nothing wrong in leaving before the inauguration, but critics blamed him for not appearing in person to hand the reins of government to his old friend and political enemy.

Chapter 5

Out of the Spotlight

Sixty-five-year-old John Adams returned to Peacefield to retire at last from public service. His son Charles had died in December of 1800 after a long struggle with alcoholism, leaving behind a wife and two young daughters. One of the daughters came to live at Peacefield with John and Abigail. Charles's widow and other daughter came often for visits. John and Abigail also enjoyed visits from their other children and grandchildren. In 1803, their son Thomas came back to live at Peacefield. He opened a law practice nearby but was miserable and unhappy. Like his late brother, he drifted into alcoholism.

The government did not yet offer pensions to former presidents so John and Abigail had to live on savings and goods they could produce on their own farmland. Adams had put money away for retirement, but his finances grew shaky. The British bank in which he placed most of his funds collapsed in 1803. To provide needed funds, John Quincy bought parts of his parents' land.

For the first time in his life, John Adams got caught up in the cycle of planting and harvesting crops. He looked forward to walking several miles a day to supervise his farm workers. In letters to friends, he boasted about his farm's increased yields.

Friends and political allies came to Peacefield to visit with the retired president, but he missed being in the spotlight. In one letter, he complained, "I am buried and forgotten." Gradually he shook off his depression and self-pity. After two years of retreat, he began to visit Boston again—for July Fourth celebrations, meetings, and Harvard affairs. He decided to write an autobiography to defend his reputation from the bitter accusations made during his presidency. After several starts and stops, he dropped the project and never completed it. He did begin to write letters to old friends, including Dr. Benjamin Rush in Philadelphia, whom he had met at the First Continental Congress. In 1806, he corresponded with Mercy Otis Warren, who had published a history of the American Revolution that was critical of Adams.

Peacefield, the house John and Abigail Adams lived in during their retirements. Today it is part of a much larger mansion created by the Adamses' children and grandchildren.

As the years passed, the Adamses became frail. Abigail was seriously ill with influenza in 1807; then a series of other illnesses followed. By 1812, she was so short of breath that it took great effort for her to speak. She also had rheuma-

tism, a painful condition that causes joints to ache. John's hands shook with palsy, which made it hard for him to write. His vision was also failing, so he had to rely on others—sometimes his grandchildren—to read to him.

John (above) and Abigail Adams (left) in old age. The portraits were painted by Gilbert Stuart, who also painted many portraits of George Washington.

Mercy Otis Warren

Mercy Otis Warren (1728–1814) was an unusual person. She was a poet, dramatist, and historian in an age when most women stayed at home and tended their families. She was a member of a leading patriot family, and her brother James Otis was the lawyer Adams had so admired as a young man. She married politician James Warren. The Adamses and the Warrens were lifelong friends.

Mercy Warren's three-volume work, *A History of the Rise, Progress, and Termination of the American Revolution*, published in 1805, is a lively account of the events of the Revolution. Warren knew many of the participants and evaluated the parts they played. She criticized Adams for being too ambitious and for favoring monarchy in America.

He wrote ten letters to her, protesting her treatment of him and denying that he was overly ambitious or favored a monarchy. Then he angrily broke off their correspondence. Nine years later, they were reconciled when Adams publicly defended her. A newspaper scoffed at Warren's claim to have written a play called *The Group* years earlier—or that any woman could write plays! Adams replied to the newspaper that he personally knew she wrote *The Group*.

☆ ☆ ☆

The old Federalist Party was losing its place as a major political force. In 1804, Thomas Jefferson was reelected, and in 1808, Democratic-Republican James Madison became president. The next year, John Quincy Adams, who had served as a U.S. senator from Massachusetts, left the Federalist Party. Only then did John Adams feel free to write more honestly about the early Federalists. He defended his presidency and criticized Alexander Hamilton and others, but soon lost interest in "rewriting history." He realized that others would have to make a final judgment on his service to his country.

In 1812, more than eleven years after Adams left the presidency, he and Thomas Jefferson renewed their friendship. By this time, Jefferson was also retired, living at Monticello, his estate in Virginia. In the remaining fourteen years of their lives, they sent each other at least 150 letters. They exchanged news about their families and sometimes commented on current events. They also tried to sort out their long-standing disagreements about politics.

Adams took renewed interest in politics during the War of 1812 between the United States and Britain. He had predicted the war and felt it would be good for the country, uniting different sections and different groups of people. When Federalists from New England gathered in Hartford, Connecticut in 1814 to object to the war and suggest that New England leave the Union, Adams criticized them severely. The Federalists' unpopular stand

The USS *Constitution*, a ship that fought valiantly in the War of 1812. John Adams was an early supporter of building a strong U.S. Navy.

on the war soon led to the destruction of the party.

The Adamses followed John Quincy's career with great pride. He was a professor at Harvard College, the first U.S. minister to Russia, and minister to Britain. In 1817, he became secretary of state in the cabinet of President James Monroe. President Monroe and his wife visited the Adamses at Peacefield in 1817.

In 1818, Abigail Adams came down with typhoid fever, a devastating illness, especially for a frail old woman. After visiting her bedside, Adams left the room and said to assembled family members, "The whole of her life has been filled up doing good. I cannot bear to see her in this state." On October 28, 1818, she died at the age of 73, just three days after the Adamses' fifty-fourth wedding anniversary. Letters of comfort arrived for John Adams from many friends, including Thomas Jefferson.

Fast Facts

THE WAR OF 1812

What: Also known as the Second War of Independence

When: 1812–1814

Who: The United States against Great Britain

Where: In the United States, Canada, and on the Atlantic Ocean

Why: Americans were angry that Britain was restricting U.S. shipping, seizing cargoes and sailors from U.S. ships, and encouraging Northwest Indians to attack American settlements.

Outcome: The 1814 Treaty of Ghent ended British impressment of American seamen and the existence of British forts in the Northwest. It extended U.S. fishing rights in Canadian waters and settled issues about naval forces on the Great Lakes and commercial relations between the two countries.

John Quincy Adams, the first son of a president to be elected president himself.
He took office in 1825, 28 years after his father.

The Final Years

For the remaining eight years of his life, Adams sorted his papers, read or was read to, and followed political developments. In 1820, he was a presidential elector, supporting the reelection of President James Monroe. He was also a delegate to the state constitutional convention, but as he noted, "I boggled and blundered." The delegates rejected his advice to add an amendment on freedom of religion to their bill of rights. The last time he spoke in public was in August 1821, when West Point cadets marched from Boston to Quincy and paraded past his home. He talked briefly to them.

In 1825, John Quincy Adams was elected president of the United States, bringing his father great joy. Jefferson wrote in February 1825, "I sincerely congratulate you on the high gratific[atio]n which the issue of the late election must have afforded you. It must excite ineffable feelings in the breast of a father to have lived to see a son to whose educ[atio]n and happiness his life has been devoted so eminently distinguished by the voice of his country."

Adams replied, "[Y]our kind congratulations are a solid comfort to my heart."

In 1826, Adams grew weaker. As July 4, the fiftieth anniversary of the Declaration of Independence, approached, Adams's doctor doubted that the

The Patriot and Diplomat

History has often remembered Adams as the patriot who was willing to defend despised British soldiers after the Boston Massacre and as a leader in the struggle to win support for American independence. Adams judged himself differently. He thought his most important contributions to the patriot cause included resisting the Massachusetts governor's plan to control the courts. Adams also pointed to his recommendation that Virginian George Washington be named commander in chief of the Continental Army, helping to create a national, rather than a regional, fighting force.

As a diplomat, Adams was one of the Americans who helped negotiate an end to the War of Independence and became the first United States minister to Great Britain. Yet Adams thought his greatest diplomatic achievement was persuading the Netherlands to recognize the new nation and to lend it desperately needed financial support.

The President

Historians have often considered Adams's presidential term a failure. In a time of great political conflict, he tried for too long to follow George Washington's example and stand above political parties. He failed to control his own cabinet or to work with Federalist Party leader Alexander Hamilton. His lack of political skills

John Adams as he looked during his term as president.

probably cost him reelection in 1800. In a letter to Thomas Jefferson late in his life, John Adams wrote,

> The real terrors of both parties have allways [*sic*] been, and now are,
>
> the fear that they shall loose [*sic*] the elections and consequently the
>
> Loaves and Fishes [rewards of office]; and that their antagonists
>
> [opponents] will obtain them.

A few days later, he explained more fully,

> I say parties and factions will not suffer, or permit improvements to
>
> be made. As soon as one man hints at an improvement his rival opposes
>
> it. No sooner has one party discovered or invented an amelioration
>
> [improvement] of the condition of man or the order of society, than
>
> the opposite party, belies it, misconstrues [misunderstands] it,
>
> misrepresents it, ridicules it, insults it, and persecutes it.

Even though he disliked the party system, Adams eventually appointed and worked with people who agreed with his political views. The federal judges he nominated at the end of his presidential term were all Federalists who shared his outlook. They continued the party's influence even after the party itself no longer existed.

Adams was also criticized for signing the Alien and Sedition Acts into law even though they violated basic freedoms. In the two centuries since Adams, other presidents have faced serious threats to national law and order and have approved similar laws. Adams's willingness to sign the acts reflected his belief that law and order are necessary for a republican government to function. It should be remembered that Adams was one of the strongest supporters of the Bill of Rights—in the Massachusetts constitution of 1780 and the U.S. Constitution.

Historians agree that Adams's foreign policy was much more successful than his achievements at home. Adams credited himself with keeping the peace, the "most splendid diamond in my crown." Even when a war against France would have been popular, he realized the huge danger war would be to the young country and successfully ended disputes with France through negotiation. At the same time, Adams was clear about the need for the United States to be prepared. He built up the navy and created a cabinet department to supervise it, realizing that sea power was more important to the United States than a standing army. In sum, he gave the country time to grow strong before the people had to fight a second war of independence in 1812.

Family Man

Even though service to his country often took him away from his loved ones, John Adams was a much admired and respected head of his family. His correspondence with Abigail over more than fifty years reflects strong and mutual affection. It is unique among the writings of American presidents.

Adams took a special interest in the education of his sons, taking them with him on long journeys through Europe and arranging for them to learn through both study and experience. He was the first president to have a son, John Quincy Adams, become president of the United States. His grandsons and great-grandsons carried on the tradition of public service well into the 1900s.

John Adams, by all accounts, could be sharp and arrogant, and he often irritated friends as well as enemies. At the end, as well as in the beginning of his long career, however, no one could doubt his deep interest in his country's welfare and his unfailing honesty.

Fast Facts   John Adams

Birth:	October 30, 1735
Birthplace:	Braintree (now Quincy), Massachusetts
Parents:	John Adams and Susanna Boylston Adams
Brothers:	Peter Boylston Adams (1738-1823)
	Elihu Adams (1741-1776)
Education:	Harvard College, A.M. degree, 1755
Occupation:	Lawyer
Marriage:	to Abigail Smith, October 25, 1764, Weymouth, Massachusetts
Children:	Abigail "Nabby" Adams Smith (1765-1813)
	John Quincy Adams (1767-1848)
	Susanna Adams (1768-1770)
	Charles Adams (1770-1800)
	Thomas Boylston Adams (1772-1832)
Political Party:	Federalist
Political Offices:	1768 Member of Massachusetts Legislature
	1774 Delegate to First Continental Congress
	1775 Delegate to Second Continental Congress
	1778 Commissioner to France
	1779 Member of Massachusetts Constitutional Convention
	1780 Minister to the Netherlands
	1785 Minister to Great Britain
	1789-1797 Vice President of the United States
	1797-1801 President of the United States
His Vice President:	Thomas Jefferson
Major Policy Decisions as President:	1798 Signed Alien and Sedition Acts
	1798 Established new Department of the Navy
	1798 Revealed XYZ Affair, kept U.S. from going to war
	1801 Appointed John Marshall Chief Justice of the Supreme Court
Firsts:	To take office in Philadelphia
	To be sworn in by a Chief Justice of the Supreme Court
	To live in the Executive Mansion
	To come from Massachusetts
	To be elected vice president and then president
	To have a son become U.S. president
Death:	July 4, 1826
Age at Death:	90 years, the second longest-lived President in U.S. history
Burial Place:	United First Parish Church, Quincy, Massachusetts

Fast Facts   Abigail Smith Adams

Birth:	November 22, 1744
Birthplace:	Weymouth, Massachusetts
Parents:	Elizabeth Quincy Smith and Reverend William Smith
Sisters and Brothers:	Mary (1741-1811)
	William (1746-1787)
	Elizabeth (1750-1815)
Education:	Home taught
Marriage:	to John Adams, October 25, 1764, Weymouth, Massachusetts
Children:	[see John Adams at left]
Firsts:	American woman presented at the British court
	Wife of an American vice president
	First Lady to live in the Executive Mansion
	First Lady whose husband and son were U.S. Presidents
Death:	October 28, 1818
Age at Death:	73 years
Burial Place:	United First Parish Church, Quincy, Massachusetts

Timeline

1735	1745	1754	1765	1767
John Adams, second president of the United States, is born.	The French Navy, at war with Britain, threatens the New England coast.	The French and Indian War begins. The American colonies and British troops oppose the French and their Indian allies.	The colonists hold a Stamp Act Congress to oppose new taxes imposed by Britain.	John Quincy Adams, sixth president of the United States, is born.

1778	1779	1783	1785	1788
France becomes an American ally and declares war on Britain. John Adams is sent to France to negotiate a treaty.	John Adams drafts a Constitution for the Massachusetts colony.	Adams is a signer of the Treaty of Paris, ending the Revolutionary War.	Adams is named U.S. Minister to Britain.	Adams returns to the U.S. The Constitution is ratified.

1797	1798	1798	1799	1800
Adams takes office in March. The U.S.S. *Constitution* ("Old Ironsides") is launched, as Adams builds up U.S. Navy.	Adams reveals that France tried to extort money from the U.S. in the XYZ Affair. Adams resists pressures for war against France.	Adams signs the unpopular Alien and Sedition Acts. 	George Washington dies.	The Convention of 1800 ends the threat of war with France. Adams is defeated for re-election by Thomas Jefferson and Aaron Burr. The government moves to Washington; the Adamses move into the Executive Mansion.

1770	1773	1774	1775	1776
John Adams defends British soldiers accused of firing on citizens in the Boston Massacre.	Parliament passes the Tea Act. Boston patriots throw taxed tea into harbor – the Boston Tea Party.	Parliament passes the Coercive/Intolerable Acts. Adams attends the First Continental Congress.	The Revolutionary War begins. Adams nominates George Washington as commander in chief of the continental army.	Adams is part of a committee that drafts the Declaration of Independence.

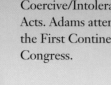

1789	1790	1792	1795	1796
Washington and Adams are elected the first president and vice president of the U.S.	The government moves from New York to Philadelphia.	Washington and Adams are reelected.	Washington signs the Jay Treaty with Britain.	John Adams is elected president; his Republican opponent Thomas Jefferson is elected vice president.

1801	1814	1817	1825	1826
The House of Representatives elects Jefferson president. Adams appoints John Marshall Chief Justice of the Supreme Court before leaving office. The Adamses retire to their home in Massachusetts.	British troops capture Washington and burn government buildings, including the Executive Mansion. In December, the Treaty of Ghent ends the War of 1812.	John Quincy Adams is appointed secretary of state by Monroe.	John Quincy Adams is elected president by the House of Representatives.	John Adams dies on July Fourth, the 50th anniversary of the Declaration of Independence. Thomas Jefferson dies the same day.

Glossary

★ ★ ★ ★

alien: a person not born in the country; an immigrant or visitor

bill of rights: a list of rights held by the people which the government pledges to protect

cabinet: the group that advises the president, made up of the secretaries (or leaders) of main government departments

candidate: a person who runs for election to a government office such as president or vice president

compromise: an agreement between groups that disagree, giving each group part of what it wants

congress: the law-making body in the United States, made up of the House of Representatives and the Senate

diplomat: a person sent by one country's government to discuss issues or negotiate agreements with another country

electoral college: the group established by the U.S. Constitution to officially elect the U.S. president and vice president

minister: an ambassador who officially represents a county to the government of another country

neutral: not taking sides in a dispute between other countries

parliament: the law-making body in Great Britain

sedition: making scandalous or false accusations against a government or against a high official

treaty: a written agreement between two countries

Further Reading

Burgan, Michael and Arthur Schlesinger. *John Adams: Second U.S. President (Revolutionary War Leaders).* Philadelphia: Chelsea House, 2000.

Gaines, Ann Graham. *John Adams: Our Second President (Our Presidents).* Chanhassen, MN: Childs World, August 2001.

Moore, Kay. *If You Lived at the Time of the American Revolution.* New York: Scholastic, 1998.

Smith, Carter, ed. *The Founding Presidents: A Sourcebook on the U.S. Presidency.* Brookfield: Millbrook Press, 1995.

MORE ADVANCED READING

Butterfield, L.H., Marc Friedlaender, and Mary Jo Kline, eds. *The Book of Abigail and John: Selected Letters of the Adams Family 1762-1784.* Cambridge: Harvard University Press, 1975.

Cappon, Lester J., ed. *The Adams-Jefferson Letters.* Chapel Hill: University of North Carolina Press, 1987.

Ellis, Joseph J. *Founding Brothers.* New York: Alfred A Knopf, 2001, pp. 206-248.

——————. *Passionate Sage.* New York: W.W. Norton & Co., 2001.

Ferling, John. *John Adams: A Life.* New York: Henry Holt, 1992.

Levin, Phyllis Lee. *Abigail Adams: A Biography.* New York: St. Martin's Griffin, 2001.

McCullough, David. *John Adams.* New York: Simon & Schuster, 2001.

Nagel, Paul C. *Descent from Glory.* New York: Oxford University Press, 1983.

Shaw, Peter. *The Character of John Adams.* Chapel Hill: University of North Carolina Press, 1976.

Weisberger, Bernard A. *America Afire.* New York: Perennial/HarperCollins, 2001.

Withey, Lynne. *Dearest Friend.* New York: Touchstone Books, 2001.

Places to Visit

Adams National Historical Park
Quincy, Massachusetts

The park includes the birthplace of John Adams and John Quincy Adams, Peacefield, the estate to which John and Abigail Adams retired, and the churchyard where the Adamses and their wives are buried.

The Federal Hall National Memorial
26 Wall Street
New York, New York
(212) 509-1595

This is the site where George Washington was sworn in as first president, with John Adams looking on.

Independence Hall
Chestnut Street between Fifth and Sixth Streets
Philadelphia, Pennsylvania

The meeting place of the First and Second Continental Congresses and the signing of the Declaration of Independence.

National Archives
Constitution Avenue
Washington, D.C.
(202) 501-5000

The White House
1600 Pennsylvania Avenue
Washington, D.C. 20500
Visitor's Office (202) 456-7041

White House Historical Association
740 Jackson Place NW
Washington, D.C. 20503
(202) 737-8292

Online Sites of Interest

★ ★ ★ ★ ★

★ **American Presidents**

http://www.americanpresident.org/kotrain/courses/JA/JA_In_Brief.htm

Provides a brief biography of Adams and much additional information on his childhood, political career, presidency, and retirement.

★ **Internet Public Library, Presidents of the United States (IPL POTUS)**

http://www.ipl.org/ref/POTUS/jadams.html

Excellent resource for personal, political, historical materials about John Adams. It includes links to other Internet sites which include places to visit and biographies.

★ **History Happens**

http://www.usahistory.com/presidents

Offers fast facts about John Adams and the text of his inaugural address.

★ **Adams National Historical Park (National Park Service)**

http://nps.gov/adam/index.htm

This site offers information about travel to, facilities at, and fees required for a visit to the Adams Historical Park, in Quincy, Massachusetts. It gives a brief description of the places of interest to tourists, such as Adams's birthplace, his home after his marriage, Peacefield, and the United First Parish Church where the President and First Lady are buried.

★ **The White House**

http://www.whitehouse.gov/WH/Welcome.html

This site provides information about the current president and vice president, a history of the Executive Mansion, virtual tours, biographies of U.S. presidents, and many other items of interest.

★ **The White House for Kids**

http://www.whitehouse.gov/kids/

Gives facts about the current president and vice president and their wives and offers descriptions of the First Family's pets. It also offers a timeline and information on timely topics of interest.

Table of Presidents

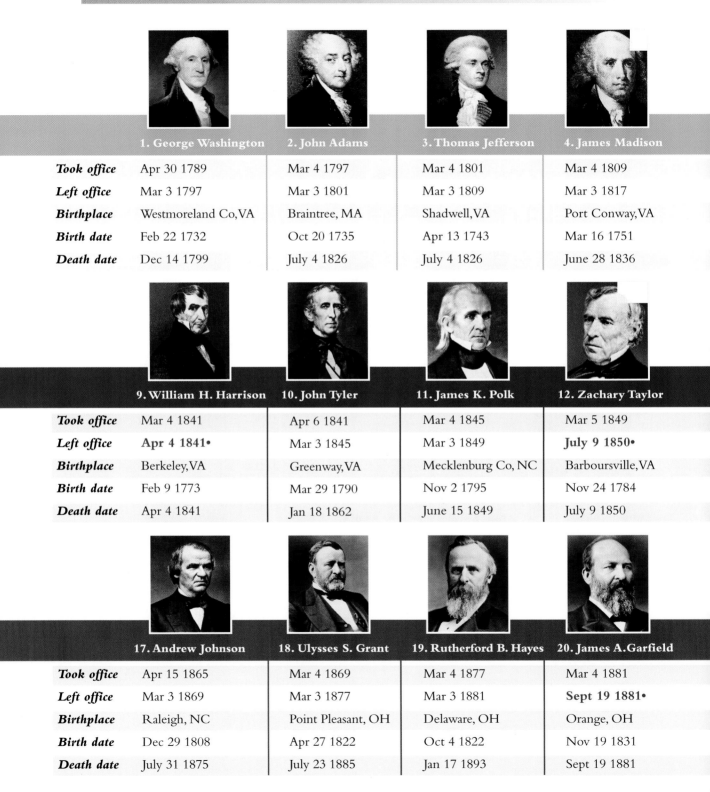

	1. George Washington	2. John Adams	3. Thomas Jefferson	4. James Madison
Took office	Apr 30 1789	Mar 4 1797	Mar 4 1801	Mar 4 1809
Left office	Mar 3 1797	Mar 3 1801	Mar 3 1809	Mar 3 1817
Birthplace	Westmoreland Co, VA	Braintree, MA	Shadwell, VA	Port Conway, VA
Birth date	Feb 22 1732	Oct 20 1735	Apr 13 1743	Mar 16 1751
Death date	Dec 14 1799	July 4 1826	July 4 1826	June 28 1836

	9. William H. Harrison	10. John Tyler	11. James K. Polk	12. Zachary Taylor
Took office	Mar 4 1841	Apr 6 1841	Mar 4 1845	Mar 5 1849
Left office	**Apr 4 1841•**	Mar 3 1845	Mar 3 1849	**July 9 1850•**
Birthplace	Berkeley, VA	Greenway, VA	Mecklenburg Co, NC	Barboursville, VA
Birth date	Feb 9 1773	Mar 29 1790	Nov 2 1795	Nov 24 1784
Death date	Apr 4 1841	Jan 18 1862	June 15 1849	July 9 1850

	17. Andrew Johnson	18. Ulysses S. Grant	19. Rutherford B. Hayes	20. James A. Garfield
Took office	Apr 15 1865	Mar 4 1869	Mar 4 1877	Mar 4 1881
Left office	Mar 3 1869	Mar 3 1877	Mar 3 1881	**Sept 19 1881•**
Birthplace	Raleigh, NC	Point Pleasant, OH	Delaware, OH	Orange, OH
Birth date	Dec 29 1808	Apr 27 1822	Oct 4 1822	Nov 19 1831
Death date	July 31 1875	July 23 1885	Jan 17 1893	Sept 19 1881

5. James Monroe

Mar 4 1817

Mar 3 1825

Westmoreland Co, VA

Apr 28 1758

July 4 1831

6. John Quincy Adams

Mar 4 1825

Mar 3 1829

Braintree, MA

July 11 1767

Feb 23 1848

7. Andrew Jackson

Mar 4 1829

Mar 3 1837

The Waxhaws, SC

Mar 15 1767

June 8 1845

8. Martin Van Buren

Mar 4 1837

Mar 3 1841

Kinderhook, NY

Dec 5 1782

July 24 1862

13. Millard Fillmore

July 9 1850

Mar 3 1853

Locke Township, NY

Jan 7 1800

Mar 8 1874

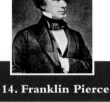

14. Franklin Pierce

Mar 4 1853

Mar 3 1857

Hillsborough, NH

Nov 23 1804

Oct 8 1869

15. James Buchanan

Mar 4 1857

Mar 3 1861

Cove Gap, PA

Apr 23 1791

June 1 1868

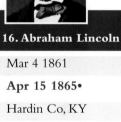

16. Abraham Lincoln

Mar 4 1861

Apr 15 1865•

Hardin Co, KY

Feb 12 1809

Apr 15 1865

21.Chester A. Arthur

Sept 19 1881

Mar 3 1885

Fairfield, VT

Oct 5 1830

Nov 18 1886

22. Grover Cleveland

Mar 4 1885

Mar 3 1889

Caldwell, NJ

Mar 18 1837

June 24 1908

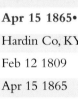

23. Benjamin Harrison

Mar 4 1889

Mar 3 1893

North Bend, OH

Aug 20 1833

Mar 13 1901

24. Grover Cleveland

Mar 4 1893

Mar 3 1897

Caldwell, NJ

Mar 18 1837

June 24 1908

	25. William McKinley	26. Theodore Roosevelt	27. William H. Taft	28. Woodrow Wilson
Took office	Mar 4 1897	Sept 14 1901	Mar 4 1909	Mar 4 1913
Left office	**Sept 14 1901•**	Mar 3 1909	Mar 3 1913	Mar 3 1921
Birthplace	Niles, OH	New York, NY	Cincinnati, OH	Staunton, VA
Birth date	Jan 29 1843	Oct 27 1858	Sept 15 1857	Dec 28 1856
Death date	Sept 14 1901	Jan 6 1919	Mar 8 1930	Feb 3 1924

	33. Harry S. Truman	34. Dwight D. Eisenhower	35. John F. Kennedy	36. Lyndon B. Johnson
Took office	Apr 12 1945	Jan 20 1953	Jan 20 1961	Nov 22 1963
Left office	Jan 20 1953	Jan 20 1961	**Nov 22 1963•**	Jan 20 1969
Birthplace	Lamar, MO	Denison, TX	Brookline, MA	Johnson City, TX
Birth date	May 8 1884	Oct 14 1890	May 29 1917	Aug 27 1908
Death date	Dec 26 1972	Mar 28 1969	Nov 22 1963	Jan 22 1973

	41. George Bush	42. Bill Clinton	43. George W. Bush	
Took office	Jan 20 1989	Jan 20 1993	Jan 20 2001	
Left office	Jan 20 1993	Jan 20 2001	—	
Birthplace	Milton, MA	Hope, AR	New Haven, CT	
Birth date	June 12 1924	Aug 19 1946	July 6 1946	
Death date	—	—	—	

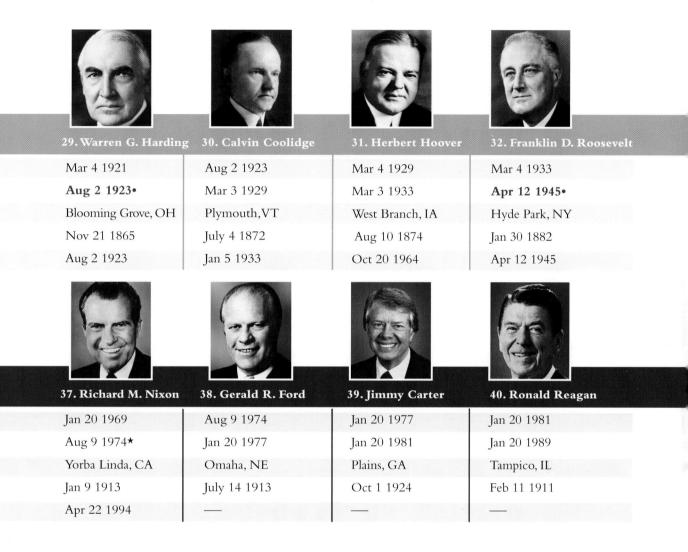

29. Warren G. Harding	30. Calvin Coolidge	31. Herbert Hoover	32. Franklin D. Roosevelt
Mar 4 1921	Aug 2 1923	Mar 4 1929	Mar 4 1933
Aug 2 1923•	Mar 3 1929	Mar 3 1933	**Apr 12 1945•**
Blooming Grove, OH	Plymouth, VT	West Branch, IA	Hyde Park, NY
Nov 21 1865	July 4 1872	Aug 10 1874	Jan 30 1882
Aug 2 1923	Jan 5 1933	Oct 20 1964	Apr 12 1945

37. Richard M. Nixon	38. Gerald R. Ford	39. Jimmy Carter	40. Ronald Reagan
Jan 20 1969	Aug 9 1974	Jan 20 1977	Jan 20 1981
Aug 9 1974★	Jan 20 1977	Jan 20 1981	Jan 20 1989
Yorba Linda, CA	Omaha, NE	Plains, GA	Tampico, IL
Jan 9 1913	July 14 1913	Oct 1 1924	Feb 11 1911
Apr 22 1994	—	—	—

• Indicates the President died while in office.

★ Richard Nixon resigned before his term expired.

Index

About the Author

Barbara Silberdick Feinberg graduated with honors from Wellesley College where she was elected to Phi Beta Kappa. She holds a Ph.D. in political science from Yale University. Among her more recent works are *Watergate: Scandal in the White House*, *American Political Scandals Past and Present*, *The National Government*, *State Governments*, *Local Governments*, *Words in the News: A Student's Dictionary of American Government and Politics*, *Harry S Truman*, *John Marshall: The Great Chief Justice*, *Electing the President*, *The Cabinet*, *Hiroshima and Nagasaki*, *Black Tuesday: The Stock Market Crash of 1929*, *Term Limits for Congress*, *The Constitutional Amendments*, *Next in Line: The American Vice Presidency*, *Patricia Ryan Nixon*, *Elizabeth Wallace Truman*, *Edith Kermit Carow Roosevelt*, *America's First Ladies: Changing Expectations*, *General Douglas MacArthur: An American Hero*, *The Dictionary of the U.S. Constitution*, *The Changing White House*, *Abraham Lincoln and the Gettysburg Address: Four Score and More*, *John McCain, Serving His Country*, *Joseph I. Lieberman: Keeping the Faith*, *The Articles of Confederation*, *John Adams*, and *Eleanor Roosevelt: A Very Special First Lady*. She has also written *Marx and Marxism*, *The Constitution: Yesterday, Today, and Tomorrow*, and *Franklin Roosevelt, Gallant President* and contributed entries to *The Young Reader's Companion to American History*.

Mrs. Feinberg is a native New Yorker and the mother of two sons, Jeremy and Douglas.